Emily Dickinson Goes Camping

Emily Dickinson Goes Camping

and Other Wildly Domestic Poems

Karen Davidson

Foreword by Marilyn Lerch

Chapel Street Editions

Appreciation of Place

Chapel Street Editions exists within the unceded and unsurrendered territories of the Wolastoqiyik, Mi'kmaq, and Peskotomuhkati people. The work we do is born from the stories carried by this land and its inhabitants. The animals, plants, soil, water, and air make this place home for the Indigenous people, who belong to this land, for the descendants of those who took this land and made it a belonging, and for those who have since come from away. Chapel Street Editions holds a deep appreciation for our place within this land and the stories it tells. We honour the land's Indigenous caretakers and are grateful for their wisdom and guidance.

Published by
Chapel Street Editions
150 Chapel Street
Woodstock, NB E7M 1H4
www.chapelstreeteditions.com
chapelstreeteditions@gmail.com

ISBN: 978-1-988299-45-7

Library and Archives Canada Cataloguing in Publication

Title: Emily Dickinson goes camping : and other wildly domestic poems / Karen Davidson.
Names: Davidson, Karen, 1948- author.
Identifiers: Canadiana 20220409374 | ISBN 9781988299457 (softcover)
Classification: LCC PS8557.A816 E45 2022 | DDC C811/.54—dc23

Book design by Brendan Helmuth

Chapel Street Editions, Ltd. gratefully acknowledges the financial support of the Department of Tourism, Heritage, and Culture, Province of New Brunswick.

New Nouveau
Brunswick

It might be easier
To fail — with Land in Sight —
Than gain — My Blue Peninsula —
To perish — of Delight

Emily Dickinson #405

Dedication

For Warren

Table of Contents

Foreword

Poets have their favourite models, influences.
I remember how liberating the long lines of
Walt Whitman were for my work, how Theodore
Roethke permitted a deeper subjectivity than
I had imagined.

It is one thing to be influenced by a poet, it is
another thing entirely to be so taken by and
intimate with a poet's technique and life that
one can create one's own voice from it. But that is
what Karen Davidson accomplishes in this book.

The first and longest section, "Emily Dickinson
Goes Camping" consists of twenty poems keyed
to various aspects of the poet's life and work. As
I crossed the threshold — no delayed gratification
here — I encountered one surprise after another,
an experience I have always found in Dickinson
as well. Whether those surprises held tears,
laughter, or longing, they always caught me
up short — "look how I surprised you."

Karen Davidson's short lines allow abrupt,
fascinating collisions of meanings and images,
as they did for Dickinson. Readers will appreciate
both the ardour and playfulness with which
the poet approaches the sacred ground of this
reclusive world and soul traveller. Brief quotes
from Dickinson's correspondence at the end of
the poems gives the reader a glimpse into her life,
providing fascinating juxtapositions.

The subtitle of this collection, "and other wildly domestic poems", promises more playfulness and paradox and old experiences remade. Karen Davidson often creates an odd and intriguing angle from which to view a poem. Her language is so self-assured she trusts the reader will find it. And though loss, old age, and death appear, there is light around them, a kind of beautiful acceptance of the many ways the world is. In our times, when many events point to dire consequences, it is comforting to read a poet who says there is yet so much to see and cherish.

Marilyn Lerch
Sackville, New Brunswick

Marilyn Lerch is the author of four volumes of poetry, including *The Physics of Allowable Sway* and *That We Have Lived At All*.

Note on Usage and Sources

Emily Dickinson signed her letters "Emilie" to various correspondents in the 1850s and 60s.

All letter quotations from *Emily Dickinson Selected Letters*, Thomas H. Johnson, Editor. The Belknap Press of Harvard University Press, 1986.

Poem quotations from *The Complete Poems of Emily Dickinson*, Thomas H. Johnson, Editor. Little, Brown and Company, 1976.

Emily Dickinson Goes Camping

Returning to Emily Dickinson

Young, I was all bounce,
delighted with bedsprings.
I asked poetry for nothing
but rhyme.
Then coming of age,
new poems became coverlets
over our bodies, his and mine,
kick one off as easily
as pull lyrics over our ears.

Cohen, McKuen, Creeley —
PK Page as cool poultice,
her Glass House Mountains
glazed in wit.
My own poetry, earnest
papier mache, its sticky verbs,
the balloon beneath
providing shape if not lift-off.

When I touched upon Emily Dickinson —
quaint and sisterly — I barely hesitated
at "It's all I have to bring today."
That meadow, those bees
freeze-dried for the next thirty years,
their buzz trapped on my bookshelf
while my children revised me.

They left and I returned.

Follow me to the ends
of The Homestead, Emily said.
So I crossed the hay field's
flowery swathes, got to where
I could look back at the skyline
and steeple — earth and sky, welded.
I should have known
by the shiver of storm on my scalp,
she'd waited.

Threshold

bees

consort in balm
one conquest at a time
hover, then
plunge into musk

bees

fill baskets
with pollen,
blossom to hive
to blossom

poet follows

under the canopy
she unties
her blue shawl
shakes it
free of petals

lingers
as though
she might yet

slip into the throat of a moonflower

Emily Dickinson Goes Camping

Emily and sister Lavinia
will go unroofed;
they'll peg their homespun
to the Common hayfield,
founding grande dames
of Adventures on an Apron String,
ox-eye daisies shared with a cow
and several stippled hares.
They'll stake their pledge
against father's bombast, mother

scolding from the pantry.
Recklessness begets a foundling,
she implies. The actual chorus:
You'll catch your death.
Sisters drag their kit outdoors
in tandem, copacetic
all their earthly lives;
a spinsterhood,
conspiring to outwit puffery.
Be still, Austin!

Tonight, bolstered in feathers,
undampened
by Amherst's rheum,
they'll trace fireflies
and constellations,
flickering
ghosts of knock-knock poems.

Who's there?

Only the moon, fleeting chaperone.

Let the suitors gather.

If Not a Herbarium

At Mount Holyoke,
while other girls rally for Jesus,
you wait for your ride;
a queue of one
at the dorm window.

Delivered home
for Thanksgiving,
you'll realize afresh
your bedroom overlooks
the burial ground.

Rejoice anyway.
What is gratitude
if not a herbarium
of salvaged petals?

In April, you'll elbow
blossoms, spout
bouquets of Latin, single out
your wild parish —

erythronium americanum:

dog's tooth violets,
adder's tongue, dappled trout
stilled in leaf shallows,
pagoda lilies;

your own meditations
fleshed
in delicate maize—

spring ephemerals.

_____

Only to think Abiah, that in 2 ½ weeks
I shall be in my own dear home again.
To Abiah Root, 1847.

Girlish Morning circa 1850

Announce myself
by stoking the fire;
Emilie at your service—
baton clanking. Thump
and rattle. Kettle drum.

Carlo's incisors
gripped to kindling—
wrest it free. Fetch!
Scoot out the open door.

Bid Hallo to Horse.
Play stamp-your-shoes
and hide the apple.

Carlo, down!

Back inside, boil
water for Mother's tea.
Eat yesterday's scone
sugared in nettles.

I remain Gooseberry—
Queen of the No-Hopes.

---

*God keep me from what they call households, except
that bright one of "faith"!* To Abiah Root, 1850.

Rosewatch

The roses bristle in their bisque vase.
Mistress is in the garden. Who's this?

An apparition hoists itself
upon the bed, snuffles with doggy
latitude, the damask covers.
Its black tail whipping,
the interloper probes
as if for truffles;
soon falls yipping into sleep.
Its dreams effuse
a diorama of Dog on the Common,
cats who need chewing out.

*

Pussy Willow remembers thorns
and springs instead
for the pillow,
claws extended.
She can smell Dog.
He's not allowed here,
but cats hoist their own flag.
Whiskers sniff the bedside table.
Puss can't resist this cloud of
gypsophila—her dainty nibble.

*

Faithful to Emily's sough of breath,
sensing high tide,
rosa gallica
turn their dreamer
toward shore.
Cat's curled under the bed.
Dog whines at the keyhole.
The roses cast off
their petals, aging and chaste.

———————————————

… With just the door ajar that oceans are … #640

Snake in the House

You may have met him, did you not
His sudden notice is ...#986

Emily's hands sink
     in bread dough,
her fingers cast
     and recast in its yeasty pillow —

a silky feel at last
     when she hears
          her sister's scream.

Green
     the fronds
          of the parlour fern,

          darker green
          its backlit spores,

          dust motes stirred
          by plank-slither —

     backbones
     braced;
          narrow fellow
     flour-dusted
     iron-stunned
apron-lifted

to the door yard where Cat lies sunning.

Heavenly Blue

My darling,
My own dear soul—
Searching for you
I set out for foreign lands

And ran aground.

How it happened
That I heard the ocean roar

I'll honor as Mystery.

Was that you, dear
Cloaked in blue

Waiting on the far shore?

On my sill, capsules
Of morning glory,
A saucer of rainwater.

Today's circumference.

...for hav'nt barques the fullest, stranded upon the shore?
To Susan Gilbert (Dickinson), 1852.

She'll Put a Trinket On

How is it she stumbles
again in the hallway?

Will she never—ever—
circumnavigate the doorstop?

quartz juggernaut
semi-precious island

grimly pearl-like—

She who ferries her heart
in a bucket of salt water.

Its jostle and slop
breaks over her ribcage.

incoming/outgoing—
bejewelled shoreline

We go out very little—once in a month or two,
we both set sail in silks…Vinnie cruises about
some to transact the commerce, but coming to
anchor, is most that I can do…
To Susan Gilbert (Dickinson), 1854.

Hide-and-Seek

One need not be a Chamber—to be Haunted—
One need not be a House—
The Brain has Corridors—surpassing
Material Place— ...#670

Emily entertains the notion of death,
constriction of vessels,
stiffening of limbs—
body a nuisance ground of decay.
And the will—ah, but the will won't give in.
Like a tree taunted
by memory of wind's last tickle,
her pen takes up where storm leaves off—
faith split, spirit daunted.
One need not be a chamber to be haunted

though stories abound in the timber frame
of hurricanes and gales at sea.
House quakes, poet eavesdrops—
if Master has sailed,
she'll horde herself.
Words will be her espoused.
Forests are felled by men, or lightning.
She alone can burn her poems—or hide them.
Her mind, a backdraft of images aroused.
One need not be a house

to flaunt fine fittings.
Light wanes—she forges her nerve.
Doors bang shut
and breath quickens. Her candle stutters.
Table steadies her hand.
Where to conceal Hope's fasting
songbird—its brittle wishbone?
In her cherry dresser, a flourish
of feathers canvassing
for breath. The brain has corridors surpassing

her father's strictures, the town's
souls dying to be saved.
Worshipping into the night,
Emily crafts her poetry
as she would a god—her own witness;
door bolted, moon effaced,
she's long since accessorized
the crow's nest.
Immortality makes its case—
poems loft beyond material place.

White Dress

Nothing fancy, straw and hay,
Bedding in a stable.
It suited fine the Babe divine—
Take comfort while you're able.

Nothing grand, no gauzy strands;
His wounds unbound, unfettered.
Why countenance superior
When inward speaks the treasure?

None of glitz, rose-stained lips,
Wayward to construe.
In winter gloom, Madonna bulb
Cocoons in fields of snow.

When will you come again, Loo? For you
remember, dear, you are one of the ones from
whom I do not run away!
To Louise Norcross, 1859.

Snowy Owl

Had I stepped
outside
in my chemise,

had I dared,

snowshoe hare
camouflaged
in winter's pale,

I might have
pointed a slipper
at my shadow,

performed a pirouette —

if not of joy
then of solidarity
with the moon.

Ah, to cavort
with like creatures
in frost dazzle —

one of a pair!

I draw myself in
baring breath
beneath the covers,

listening
for the owl—
tunneling like the mole.

---

*I am older—tonight, Master—but the love is
the same—so are the moon and the crescent. ...*
To Master, about 1861.

Pens and Needles

Midnight's ledger
inked in attar of roses,
maids and groomsmen.

Bride's crème de la crème!

But I blush at my pen's
inhibitions. Not bride.
Merely a celebrant

in funereal crepe —

that vile Whitman
blandishing his green
encouragements.

Who invited his ilk?

With fancy's remnant,
I'll stitch a reprisal;
gossamer skirt, gilly

flowers strewn on
bodice — my own, of course.
Sleeves crimped for

immortality's reach. Cuffs
I might once have let down,
turned and pinned
in a brazen fluster of hands,
O My Master!

Born—Bridalled—Shrouded—In a Day— ...
To Samuel Bowles, 1862.

Bivouac

Ladybirds
scout my wallpaper.

Flies fiddle taps
on the pane.

Robins seek
a quorum of worms.

And I can't
tell the crocuses
anything —

already they've
mustered
mauve and yellow —

no mind for Almanac snow.

The Wind blows gay today and the Jays bark like Blue Terriers ... To Mrs. J.G. Holland, early March 1866.

Eye Trouble

Though advised not to, my eyes
met noon's glare
with the temerity of fledglings.

When I loosened my upheld hair
and leaned forward,
tortoise shells clattered to the floor.
I bathed in a light
auburn as robin's breast
in winter's austere. Its parting —
a deadbolt drawn back — was a river
flung wild and fierce

into the shade pool of myself.

Eyes escaped upwards
astonished at the white doll below,
doubled over in prayer.

*…what indeed is Earth but a Nest, from whose
rim we are all falling?*
To Mrs. J. G. Holland, 1879.

The Niceties

We were happy, Emily,
you found love late in life;
how one of your father's
old boys caught
at the starched hem
of your house dress.
How you relented
perhaps even giggled,
one mother-of-pearl
button at a time.

Were you coy and/or
merely grateful
for the delicacy
of a man's touch?
Judge Otis Lord's,
widower
who could not set
a foot wrong
but that he succumbed
to a heart attack,
sweet rascal,
not long after
he first wooed you.

Myth of Amherst,
were you able
to see just once
Judge Lord step out
of his trousers
with the sole purpose
of lying next to you?
You, who might have shed
your white habit
to emerge in his arms
fragrant
with the dusty talcum
of etiquette?

I have a strong surmise that the moments we
have not known are tenderest to you...
To Otis P. Lord, 1882.

Reputation

If fascination begins
as meadow-lust
for happy endings,

ambition too
must rise in the world.

Lavinia relinquished
bundles of Emily's poems
to Austin's mistress —

ingénue editor — who ordered,
transcribed, published
The Myth's scribbles.

Mabel chose
her own painting —
Indian Pipe — as portal

to the 1890 First Edition.

Strategic — albeit saprophytic —
finger prints on white dimity.

---

*I still cherish the clutch with which I bore
(Indian pipe) from the ground when a
wondering child...*
To Mabel Loomis Todd, 1882.

Martha Remembers Aunt Emily

Though ghostly in white,
the Myth was our red-haired imp —
her spatula quick as her tongue.

Can you see children jostling
below her window? That was us.
Aunt Emily was our lofty spy

dangling gingerbread in a basket —
mind the hummingbirds!
We ate, not out of her hand,

but with upturned eyes.

Doting Auntie clapped,
then wept for Gilbert's birthday parade —

our baby brother, Gib, just eight,
died from typhoid fever.

Aunt Emily withered.

Father's hand tipped
in the direction of Mrs. Todd
who by offering to edit

our deceased Aunt's verse

(Was there no end to it?)

force-fed Father's treason
past Mother's black veil;
my own clenched teeth.

With two dead brothers,
and a father buried
in his hussy's skirts, I returned

as the "Imperial Girl"
Aunt Emily had once crowned me.
Her manuscripts, surrendered,

were disputed territory
with no one left to defend them,
but her dogged niece, Mattie.

All the While

Fiction moved her; she read widely,
became soul-sister to the Brontës
by cruising the moors. She could
afford to. She was so well-connected,

she embodied her own entourage;

first daughter of Amherst, head
gardener and pen pal, nursemaid
to her hothouse mother; Lover
of Words. The poet's choice —

demur from exhibiting her roses,
send missives to pot marigolds
begging their pardon.
Who could feed her fervent brain

but her own alter ego? Hardy orchid
who calypsoed in the Rockies;
as much undertow as ecstatic bee-bower,
Appalachian meadow as burial at sea.

Was it the wild or domestic Emily
charted the Reverend Wadsworth's
sea voyage through shoals of loss —
abridged Panama by leaving her door ajar?

Piping Plover

charadrius melodus

Unremarked, sand-stayed,
until the mourners crouched;
verse candled for Eternity.

You didn't ask for much.

Your silver-winged
reconnaissance
isolate in the air;

trinkets of bravado —
more than souls can bear,
who saunter shores deserted

or teem in city's glitter.
Tread each day unpoetical —
but for the eggshell twitter.

Compass

The Tangled Garden

How long before
MacDonald reached
for his paintbrush,
having waited most of August
for the sunflowers
to tilt their spotlights?
Did he chase off jays
and neighbourhood children?
Did he encounter a cat?

Each season
re-arranges palette and canvas;
today the viewer
is held at bay,
like a dun-coloured
dog on a radiant leash.
Either stand to one side
in the gallery

or pace the periphery

where what lies
beyond the feeder blurs;
now rogue sunflowers
lose sway

to a rain forest
of bougainvillia
and what I long to be
hothouse orchids,
lime green and clingy.

It's winter out there.

I've stepped in to find my toad.

After visiting J. E. H. MacDonald's "The
Tangled Garden" at the National Gallery in
Ottawa—in January.

Weasel

for Annie Dillard

Even camouflaged
in a fern-strewn forest,
I'm afraid your prose
might tease me out,
push me over the cliff.

Unlike your Chilean
softwoods, stunted
into survival,
comfort is my hearthstone.
I've ordered firewood.

So many edges
has your world, so much
fervor that won't back down—
that wants to tear
a strip off
to make me whole.

Where will I live, Annie,
if you call me out?
Whose is this
black-tipped tail frozen
hard in the snow?

Help Line

When told quietly by the Great Unknown,
You'll never see spring again, I replied,
How would you know? He said, at the very least,
spring's unlikely. If I were you,
I wouldn't count on it. Fill your rubber boots
with house plants. Keep your mukluks handy.
No raincoats unless you have one of those
all-weather numbers with the zip-out lining.
Chances are slim you'll be zipping out soon.
Oh, he said, and gloves. Don't even think
of trying on those leather-palmed workers
with the neon green thumbs. What you want now
are the polar specials, lined
with lemmings who thought like you;
winter was finite, spring would arrive,
you'd emerge half-naked on the clam shell of escape.
Instead they raced to the sea and look
where it got them. Hello?

Compass

January can't make up its mind.
The depression cupping
wildflowers and grasses
filled with snow yesterday.
Today, it's a swimming pool.
Beside its ripples, miscanthus
and trembling bee balm.

Dog and I skirt the edges
of this latest body of water—
uncharted territory.
Our previous dog, a Labrador,
would be wading by now;
that violent shirk
of droplets after
he came clean, a little hasty.
I'd have jumped back, too late.
I miss his freedom.

This one's leashed. He sniffs
and yearns. I shuffle.
Once water freezes
to a murky looking glass,
we'll step out and practice our spins.
My wobbled axis—an old dog
and a young dog
running circles around me.

Charm Bracelet

Scratched in window frost, her brief
spell of denial might look and smell
like lilacs in full throttle...or Golden Gate
Park, its tea garden; late March
water-colour for little mother on sabbatical.

Under a revolving parasol of cherry
blossoms, her face hidden by one hand,
the other writing haiku — ostensibly —
but who would know? Light rain
washes her lines into inky branches
extended to the children she's left behind.

Her body's in San Francisco with their father.
Her body is as happy as it will ever be.

A charm bracelet of Manitoba maple keys
cuffs her pale wrist. They'll grow anywhere.
Now as she looks up, she sees her life
partner in the blossom mist
and a baby with red-gold curls, yet to be born.

Cherry blossoms whorl into pasque flowers;
branch-end nodes will burst
crocus upon her return — prairie rebirth.

Fair Trade

Morning turns over,
sky mottling
blue-grey like old skin
or thin milk.

November grabs hold —
liniment wind
and hand-wringing.

Ferreting out mitts
and hoods,
socks Father might once

have worn to the barn,
nubbly wool;
commodious boots.

Wind tunnels
under raised collars;
remember our

teenaged fingers
roofed over earlobes?
Snow served on a shovel,
blown into our faces.

Where are we again?

Noon's inside lane,
sink to wood stove,
birch bark crackling.

...Café au lait,
melted chocolate,
instant espresso ...no, my darling.

Froth of chai latte
rimming our mouths.

Once You Bloomed

for Sylvia Plath

June, month of rosy delirium and bees.
Narcissus bulbs, tissue-wrapped,
snugged in Devon humus, foliage
all but ripened when your spade
demanded returns; earth-clinging wombs,
multipliers. Dozens of fitful sleepers
gorging under the pinks.

You'd barely taken ownership
when the phone rang. Your final
months wrested and plea bargained;
abundance became loss.
Husband-loss. Father-loss.

You became homeless again.

You picked your way to the BBC
musky-voiced, flu-plagued, your satchel
of spring pleasures banished
to the novitiate of first loves.
These new poems were muck-coated.

But breathing. Still breathing.

You'd knelt among the narcissi
with your babies: look at you, luv.
Poeticus, your delicate eye,
forever rain-lashed.

Fish in Her Garden

Heron's slip?
Unlikely.
She'll pin the blame
on their house cat—
be-header of rabbits,
silencer of song birds.
Nowhere to be seen.

At her feet,
fin-flutter,
flabbergast.
Trout, little
more than a parr;
river, little more
than a brook.

Must have been
a quick catch;
tabby flanks
parting reeds,
eyes fixed
on the shallows—darting
shadow.

Trout mistakes
paw
for an alder root;
claw
hooks home.

Journey uphill
to her garden—

brain food.

Poppies

The Verge

High bush cranberries
hang as if dejected
to be considered only
after the brash clusters
of mountain ash
have been depleted.

Sumac's velvety horns
are gone by
morning's light;
someone has nibbled
overnight
their cushioned fruit.

And what of these
brown-red
berries of blood—
the blood-smeared
depression
in the snow?

Winter's reds
arrest the eye,
startle the heart
into asking

Where did I go wrong?

Covered Bridge

Kennebecasis River; #23 Malone Bridge
at Goshen. Built in 1910; length, 58 feet.

Piebald pulls them
through creak and shadow,
tremolo of two young
bodies' shallow
breathing, moving
deep into 1914.
He leaves tomorrow
for Camp Sussex.

Horse slows, "Whoa, there."
Lantern flickers.
The boy, who is eighteen,
won't be deterred.
He reaches for her,
soft bristle above his lips
tickling her cheek.

His voice quiet and deliberate,
her nervous laughter;
she'd like to change
the subject.

"I won't be gone long, you'll see."

Beyond his shoulder,
the opening … the moonlight.

Sheet Lightning

My uncles came back bloodied
and not yet ready to quit.
At twilight, they slouched
around our wheat field, smoking.
Most of them had been soldiers
in the infantry, in the air.
Why shouldn't they return
to inhabit the night terrors of a young niece?

I stood apart watching them take aim
at boys from my school.
They all wore the same uniforms.

I could only count to twenty.

No one would leave though
I asked politely.
A kid in Punkinhead pyjamas,
I tried pleading.
My father always brought me
water when I called out.

Where was he?

I heard the rumble of planes.
Then a haystack exploded.
Easter lilies caught fire, beacons
along the headland's corridor.

I ran to tell my grandmother
where her boys were, the ones
who came back from the war.

Tea Caddy

Cups in hand, we feel embraced—
arms that held us once,
a story we need to continue.

Our Irish grandfather went so far
as to bake his own soda bread.
Grandma Myrtle boiled the kettle.

My mother delivered hot tea
in Mason jars to Dad and his cousin
harvesting wheat in early autumn.

My mother-in-law, Irene, studied
her tea cup; amongst the roses,
a North Atlantic minesweeper

moved towards the rim, Halifax.
She and her firstborn, little Kenneth
waited off Dutch Mill Road.

Irene saw in the tea leaves
what she wanted to see;
Kenny returned.

The three of them rode the train
back to the prairies. In her belly,
the boy who became my husband.

Snow Feast

Should you, a gypsy child,
have turned up on my farm
in deepest winter
(you, lover and I, who've
played at keeping house, who still try);
should you have stolen over a snow bank
and proposed outright,
"Let's build a fort and get married",
I would have plodded after you,
a bride in frost-caked mittens;

would have dug through thickest drifts
for shards of grandmother's
Blue Willow china to set our table,
burrowed trenches and braved thorns
to seek rose-hips for a centrepiece.

Nothing much has changed.

Resourceful to a fault,
I might have searched the deep freeze
for summer's mud pies,
having discreetly
        counted the urchins
hiding behind your black diamond eyes.

Late August Reel

In Theodore Roetke's poem,
"My Papa's Waltz," Teddy strides
atop his father's work boots
and sways, years later, to gusts
of his whisky breath.

I never danced with my father—
not once—unless it was
to sweep out a granary in dusty
unison, a line dance of sorts.

All our own—all I had—
never having invited an orchestra
or even one accordion
to my wedding with Warren.

Dad and I in late August,
chaff skirling;
and on this rare occasion
our corn brooms—
not our voices—raised.

The Night Before You Left

In my dream, you walk in your sleep
as you did the night before you left
for Rwanda.

You wander into a camp
of armed tribesmen, following
the death cries of babies,
their mothers' moans.
You embrace each one —
the soldiers
who are children,
the children
who are corpses,
the corpses
whose mothers wail eternally.

You lean into them, are one of them —
I wait in our bedroom doorway,
hear the first footfall on the stairs.

It's you —
they haven't killed you after all.

You teeter
on the landing
and tumble
backwards into Kigali Stadium.

I wake up. You've been talking
in your sleep, calling for your mother.

Poppies

I've never fed them.
What would they eat?

wraithes in red petticoats,
ephemerals striking

poses for an hour or two
scattered to winter

bee balm and you —
ghostly infantry

until *corps de ballet* —
they torch the Bastille

petals&poppyseeds&petals
& poppy seeds

What did they eat?

Just for Tonight

Let me be witch hazel
to your hemlock.
Let's lope into the hills,
willow-limbed
and eager — as though
there will always
be someone
who considers us beautiful.

Let's audition
wood frogs, sort croaks
from quacks. Let ducks
collude even as we ride
the swollen water,
lunging
where it slides
over Pleasant Mountain,
leaping

where it pools at our feet.

My neck
will welcome
your scarf
of old man's beard. I'll —

but you're not looking.

The stars swarm in the river
and I can't be sure
we'll find each other again.

Twenty Years

for Denise, again

Her straw yellow house
rested on the edge of a cliff—
cliff being too
extreme a word
for an embankment; yet
what do you call
a land form that devolves
into a drop-off?

A dead end.

A car once flew
over the tansy
railing, and its occupants,
whoever they were,
climbed
out of the wreckage.

Our family dwelled
in a tall brick house at an angle
across the street.
When we tapped on our
sunroom window,

Denise would look up
from her bicycle and wave,
her head, her hand
raised and her wide
mouth smiling,
taking in all the air
of an autumn day before the diagnosis.

Denise.

We loved you for that wave;
in these twenty years since,
you've never ceased
waving and smiling;

we won't let you.

Farm Team

Butterfly House

In early April, sap rising,
swelling buds
nudge last year's beech leaves
just as monarchs,
wintering in northern Mexico,
embark *en masse*—

memory's air stream.

On our prairie farm,
they'll cling to honeysuckle
or caragana or little
girls' stubby fingers
daubed in nail enamel.

Mother's green kid
gloves already split
into finger puppets;

tattle tales. Katydid chorus.

Four daughters, one

bathroom: cramps,
blunted lipsticks, Kotex pads.

Who will emerge and when?

Our father wants to know.

The Back Seat

The snapshot shows us standing beside a four-door
sedan, circa 1950.

Grandma holds her terrier, Aylmer, whose curly-
haired coat matches the little girl's head—the same
head that became a fractured skull in a car accident
months later. The story goes that after Aylmer bit
this child on the nose, he became known as The
Little Brute. Perhaps Grandma considered her
granddaughter a little brute for provoking Aylmer.
She might have said so.

Well, maybe the old lady would have to take her
damn dog and leave. Grandmother and dog moved
into Stonewall—must have been shortly after

Mom took the picture—leaving behind toddler
and mother, father and farm. Grass probably snuck
into Grandma's perennials, just as my mother edged
out her mother-in-law as woman of the house.

That fall, hearing about the accident, did Grandma
weep in her rented room at Nel Stinson's? Did she
wonder how they could have let it happen? Her first
grandchild half-dead on a gravel road.

Had Aunt Betty screamed, " Karen's fallen out of the car"?

Studying the picture, I want Grandma with me in the back seat, the plump upholstery of her arms holding on. Instead, the door handle gives and I'm flying into a past I don't remember.

My Skating Dream

Dick is not the still life in a brown
pasture; round draft horse retired
by my father, predeceased by Silver.

I am not the skinny girl shivering
in Grace Borthistle's scuffed
figure skates, reminding my ankles

to brace themselves.

Together, Dick and I are Sub-Zero,
Rime of Legend, led on by
Arcturus, windswept; our cutter

chases the moon over an ice-bald dome.

When the mood strikes, I step out
in my warm skates. Dick shrugs off the reins
and prances alongside. He gesticulates

like Brian Orser coaching. (At heart,
Dick remains a working horse
whose hooves happen

to be back lit by the aurora.)

Before long, all my ankles can muster
is a bunny hop, over and over, a filigree
chain I'm feeding with my scissor blades,

back to bed.

Dick parks the cutter in the evergreens
where nobody else can find it.
Brian Ostler leads him into the barn.

Gold Mettle

1948 Winter Olympics, St. Moritz

The day before—a tracery of nerves.
Barbara Ann Scott laced up, donned her angora helmet
to skate School Figures—loop change loop—repeat.

Free Skate was delayed until next afternoon;
warm weather, slushy ice. "I could have worn
a bathing suit and been entirely comfortable."

She had but one costume—fur. She drew #13.
A rival fell three times in the sinkholes
from two previous hockey games.

"B.A., the ice is just terrible." She'd been warned.

B.A. scarcely touched down.

Her spirals nailed an angel's wingspan

                    her stag jump soared over the boards

        her back-bend spin orbited a

        Gold Medal.

Home in Ottawa, Barbara Ann was presented
with keys to her buffed-new Buick roadster.

License plate 48-U-1

———————————

Quotations from Skate with Me, *Barbara Ann
Scott, Doubleday, 1950.*

Track and Field

Dad's Minneapolis Moline
had already made tracks.
If I'd passed the combine shed
I would have followed
his tractor's well-worn path.
But my circuit that spring was as new
as my plan to win
the 100-yard dash at the district track meet.

I warmed up with wide-legged bows,
the barn upside down
between my knees.
More stretches, jumping jacks,
then a tentative pounding — black dust
threatening my canvas runners —
up on the ball of each foot.
Now wind sprints —
slow, fast, slow, faster.
Slow. Bees in the alfalfa, my lips
blowing out stale air.

Dad's tractor steady past the headland,
jerky tide in my chest.

Who's this? The dog
play-snapping at my heels.
Hi Boy—brush a hand
over his ear, wipe my face on my sleeve.
Turn around, trip over dog
now rocking on his back in the dust,
paws waving at the sky.
He's come undone—something
my bashful track coach, Mr. Clym
would never do.

Unless I won the 100-yard dash.

Lemon Meringue Pie

1. Mom always said if you want
another piece, eat everything.
Don't just scoop out the filling
and leave the crust. By the way,
too flakey's as bad as tough.
Crust's a foundation garment.

Never a crinoline.

2. Make lemon curd slightly tart,
neither sweet nor sour; err on sweet.
Be patient while stirring.
Turning up the heat leads to chaos.
Better to turn up the hi fi.

Nat King Cole. Not Peggy Lee.

3. Meringue shouldn't weep.
If it breaks out in tears,
you've hurt its feelings
by not whisking in the sugar
one tablespoon at a time. Or by not beating
into folds that stand on their own.

Or, God forbid, piling on warm curd.

Wait.

4. Swirl with precision,
making sure you come in contact
with the fluted pastry rim.
Tan your pie briefly in the oven,
rest at room temperature, out of reach
of zealots and cats. Lift and plate

in a flourish of modesty...Act surprised.

Mother's Day

Faced with the humble potato,
daughter looks deep into its inset eyes,
dreams earthy, not sea, scallops;
imagines her mother peeling Pontiac
after Pontiac, a couple of burly onions,
deliberately slicing
then arranging supper's lineage
in a burnt orange casserole,
potatoes-onions-potatoes—
flouring, seasoning each layer
plumped with pats of butter.

Her name was Pat.

Mom made the best potato scallop:
cow's milk expressed
from the barn, courtesy of our father;
spuds we'd been coerced into picking
in mitten weather, now
cresting golden, potholders ditched.
All hands on deck, mouths
off to the races. Nothing left but the dish.

Reaching for My Father

The first difficulty—overcoming the distance
between his Alberta and my Albert County,
New Brunswick. He's eighty-four, fragile as flax
in October, and he's likely lost my name forever.
"The oldest", he called me in the hospital. After
I'd flown back east, he asked my youngest sister,
Are you the oldest?

"Why aren't you taking me home?" he asked
as she turned to leave. To another sister, he
demanded, "Take me home." They don't want to
visit him anymore. They know they can't take him
home in that body. The resources that kept him
on the land have been exhausted. It's November.
The granary's empty. Snow is falling.

I'm reaching for the father who kept us warm,
but never supplied enough words; whose face was
turned from the ice and wind, never away from
his children; whose eyes were the rapid shutter
blue of flax blossoms; the open-mindedness
I never read until much later. It was as if he
appraised and weighed each thought. Click.

I reach over the phone to where he lies in
hospital. To my endless questions, abbreviated
yesterday to, "How are you, Dad?" He replies,
"You're the oldest, aren't you? Come and get me."

Come to Rest

Below me, in the Rockwood Cemetery, lie the bones
of my maternal grandmother and grandfather, my
Uncle Charlie at their feet, cremated-to-measure
all these years later. Uncle Charlie, who'd been
groundskeeper here when I was a teenager, seems to
hover still, as if waiting for us to depart. I am never
sure on these brief flights in where to land, each of
us sidestepping strangers.

Our mother has let it be known that she doesn't
want to be buried here. Nor will she rest out at
St. Michael's where her husband's family sleeps
next to the grain fields. Rather, once she passes, she
wants to stay put in Alberta. Could be that one big
move was enough for her. She and Dad retired to
Camrose, leaving Uncle Charlie to tend to himself;
hadn't Grandma left all of her money to Charlie and
Bill, the poor bachelors? Mom's bitter pill, savoured.

In the meantime, Dad has died, his ashes planted in
the shadow of his parents' tombstone.

Mom's cutting her losses.
Don't bury me in Manitoba, she says.
I won't come back.

Farm Team

Traded to Wainwright,
our mother
was out of her league.
How we wished she could have
stick-handled her minders,
making her way on her own blades
not just down the hall to supper,
which she invariably poked at,
but to the bathroom, unassisted.
She who loved the rough and tumble
of the tongue, a high sticker,
couldn't see her way around the remote.
We muted the "Hurry Hard"
of curling, clicked fielder's choice,
gathered her in our arms
and tried to carry her over the finish line —
another residence closer to home,
intensive care.

She left on her own.

I doubt now I appreciated
her game enough, confusing
both of us as referee/censor.
I wish she knew,
even if I forgot sometimes,
we played for the same team.

Sister Porcupine

Our antiquated hips
and halting gait
were no match for the black Lab
whose nose came this close
to doubling as pincushion.
When we threw him a biscuit,
he backed off.

We studied a crab apple,
climbed its tree,
turned our backs on enemies.

The quiet of resting
in our basket of quills
was short-lived.
One of the guys in the house
wanted to shoot us.
A neighbour blamed us for killing
his pine trees.
A vet's bill was still possible.

Two days ago, the mini van.

Only the crow knows where I left you.

Lambs' Wool

Wind howls, high-strung
and mindless,
scattering its buckshot.

Glass takes on a life.
Lantern-glow dissolves
a woman's features.
Her warm breath
seals the earthen walls.

So the weaver cards her wool.

So the sleeping man
dreams a flock of wolves.

The Best Light

Christmas Eve, the Veranda

Roof-water drips
as icicles elongate; moonlit,
mysteriously lucid,
reflecting a reflection.
Is this the first night
of the rest of your life, Jesus? ... Again.
Each year, the murmur of strangers,
beasts shuffling in the straw,
hands wrapping you close and closer.

Can you move,
for all those swaddling clothes?

Must you accelerate
towards daybreak, babbling baby-speak
in forty-seven languages,
learn to mouth
the vowels: I. Owe. You? ...
What do you owe us
rough-hewn thinkers
gathered on the veranda?

The farm, you owe us the farm —
your green umbilical cord
attached to this night;

our bright cultivators
twanging the stars,
the earth in harness.

The barn isn't burning yet, Jesus,
and we aren't falling.
Catch us up anyway, hold us down.
Wish upon us.

Ramshackle

Weather pried the shed open
and spit it out,
one grey shingle at a time.

Once it held chickens
that scratched their way
into its being; clucking,
carrying on all night
so the shed was hard-pressed
to remember the forest.
It only lived to shut up chickens.
Or let in the farmer's wife.

But as its floorboards
swayed to the Rhode Island two-step,
they admitted the weasel
and more open-spirited—the raccoon
who fondled and crushed eggs
in her cupped paws.
The weasel shook residents
by their scruffs, sucked
their squawks.

The farm wife gave up.
The shed's roof gave in.

Some nights I swear
I hear a broody hen
objecting to the indignities.

Micro-Climate

A terrarium of sorts; Mason jar wedged
in the shale and rubbish of the cottage
where Emma and Alden lived their last
contentious years together.

The jar, settled lengthwise,
admitted moss and sticks, one straggly fern
and a grove of grey-green lichens.
I imagine plethiosaurs, or at the very least
dragon flies escaping its misted walls.

Instead, a yellow-spotted salamander
leaps to its freedom. I scream.

Somewhere, Emma fumes at the effrontery
of nature and/or my squeamishness.
At least it's not one of his whisky bottles.
How she wishes her last years with Alden

had been different; evidence he deposited
Lord knows where. Admit it, Emma, there
in the day lilies. He came to like gut-rot
more than time with his wife, one of
the original Gray sisters from over-home.

Emma's preserves, but for the clouded
terrarium, outlasted a slew of winters.
Emma survived Alden's ungodly thirst
to enjoy leftovers in a county nursing home.

But Who's Counting?

It might have been on the radio he heard
that alcoholics in Scandinavian rehab
were given two, and up to four, apple ciders a day,
surely for cider's good taste,
also as withdrawal prevention. Who can say
cider doesn't cheer a person up?
A consideration so often overlooked
with those who drink to excess,
those who've seen enough, who've found
a way to medicate pain for days on end.

But who's counting except the recyclers?

It's possible these onlookers
should likewise be gifted with several
ciders a day, no bitterness, no false cheer;
just the leisurely intake of fermented apple
on a day of no particular consequence
except someone thought you might need a lift.

How are You?

The collapse of shoulders, dislocation
of conversation when drugged
by pain-killers, he tells her
Lady Ashburton arrived last night
for some heavy drinking—
he and Barney and Lady Ashburton
tippling gimlets of gin? Home brew?

What were you drinking?

Pickle juice, he replies,
with a sly grin.

Emma checks her own pulse.

How am I?

Who's asking? Shoulders rise and fall
in the semblance of a shrug.
It's not that Emma doesn't know or care,
only she's out of sorts—
one of many ladybirds
attracted to east-facing windows.

Now they can't find their way out.

Capital "M" for Milkweed

Do hobbyists still stick pins in butterflies
or press flowers but to flared nostrils?

Who today sends impassioned poems
unless with thumbs or trigger fingers?

Roadsides, power lines, tree plantations,
fields; blanket coverage. Matching

corn stalks, softest ass-wipe spruce.

Monarchs audition as nature's postage stamps.

Erstwhile calligraphers —

illuminated footnotes to the bottom line.

Building on Sand

It's all a matter of moons,
she might say.
Their waxing and waning
pulls
tide over sand like a wet blanket.

For now, our castle could use
embellishments—
shells and ocean-smoothed quartz,
gull's feathers, and how about
our wish bone
picked clean as a window arch?

On this bright August day
of cold chicken, shouts
of Watch Out and My Turn
and Here They Come
meet encroaching waves.

Walls won't hold.
                    Turrets wash away.

Children, resigned, turn
towards home,
a little defeated. And the dog,
retrieved from befriending strangers—
how could they
forget Daisy,
belching seawater
over buckled-in shoulders?

Conkers

Flung over escarpments,
left behind
in darkened rough,
Aging Gardener's new tools
should find their own way home,
cheerfully blinking
On and Off.

Their ergonomics
should coax her.
Use your wrists wisely—
trowel steadied, each transplanted
morning within your grasp.

Her spade's curvature
should ease her stooped back.

And should she tread
lead-footed on the tines
of her rake, let it radiate
shooting stars
and soothe
her earthly peccadilloes
with birdsong.

Oh! Then she'll lean
refreshed
into her dance partner, Hoe,
and gleefully
whack the dickens out of the chickweed.

Bespoke

My walk-around—apple tree
to tree: most gnarled, unnamed,
inherited with our move.
Which branches are crossed
or out of reach for the picker?
Are any broken and/or diseased?
And truthfully,
which generous old producers
—Yellow Transparents—
will rot unappreciated?

Timely pruning
(before leaves appear in April)
will lighten the windfall.

Once I've sized up the trees,
I call upon our son—
chain saw wielder.
Pruning's his spring training.
I coach, hands gripping stepladder.
Patrick ascends, reaching,
forsakes the chainsaw.
For the more delicate cuts,
he uses a fine hacksaw
that was his father's;
a father who may have told him

the sharpest blades
require the keenest eyesight.

Spring's when we realize a task
may yield the deepest
and most meaningful of pleasures.
It's all in the preparation.

The Best Light Used to Be

for Stefan

The best light used to be early
morning or evening—
still is, though digital's messed
with the significance of timing ...

Fuss enough with Photoshop
you'll get your shot, right?

So if light's an afterthought ...

We admired how you held your Canon
to the blue scillas this morning
before they ran
to their small ruin in the dew.

Or tonight ... When sun hijacked
the riverbank and maple's
thousand-fold ruby tassels

shimmered a ransom note . . .

You gave that tree everything you had—

light's five-minute arsenal.

Blue Studio

Muscari, also known as grape hyacinth

If my body shields the page as *sanctum*,
then my window's strung with fairy lights.

Whimsy's pinpricks.

At my right shoulder, The Blizzard;
inquisitive flicks steel themselves.

Wind begins to keen.

Somebody's dog—possibly a coyote—
has slipped on ice. Splayed on all fours,

he may have fallen in.

On my warm side, pots of muscari
are staged to bloom. Sequestering

the bulbs, I imagined

white and blue bonnets collaged
on black construction paper.

Artist's proof.

While my recording arm registers cold,
my free hand cradles grape hyacinths.

Carlo looks up.

Lines Towards a Haiku

Maybe it was the BBC episode
on Japanese cherry blossoms
downloaded as inspiration
in the (still) dark corridors.
The ancient discipline for shaping
growth within the confines
of available space; preserve the view.

My vantage point, one day into spring,
tells me the oak in its adolescence
could use a spruce-up;
limbs elongated, weeping into snow,
acorns' merry elf beanies strewn.
Oak's been scarred.
Bullet-ridden by a sapsucker.

Hawthorn groans unchecked —
criss-crossed panoply. To reach
with loppers is to chop
at a woody octopus, one limb drops
and a third or fourth
screws my shoulder with thorns.
Short-lived ardour. Know when to quit.

The blackberries. Make-work project
I should have prioritized in fall.
Here come our grandchildren,
gauntleted — how long will they last
stripping last year's broken canes?
Old sticklers versus
Gran's lippy labour market. For now.

Visions of berry baskets, heaped.

Apples at last, their decrepit claim
to heritage, knuckled under February
ice rain; vestige of first families
herding cows for twice-daily milking;
notion of flawless fruit long since
put to pasture
until next spring's blossoming …

Annapolis bees
knee-deep in pink pantaloons;
life in our old girls.

Afterword
Poem Upon Poem

"God keep me from what they call households!" So wrote twenty-year-old Emily Dickinson to her friend Abiah Root in 1850. While she may have remained aloof from scrubbing and dusting—those seemed to be her sister Lavinia's domain—she nevertheless lived in the family's homes in Amherst, Massachusetts from cradle to grave. Emily's was, by modern standards, a very stationary existence, unless you count the almost 1800 poems she wrote from the fo'c'sle of the good ship, Imagination.

As an adolescent she'd run the meadows collecting and drying wildflowers for her herbarium. She'd gone on skating junkets and woodland hikes with her dog, Carlo. She was a wild child when given the chance. She might even have gone camping within, and without, town limits.

Emily Dickinson ventured on the stormy seas of Faith, exploring what to believe of religious doctrine, what to anticipate—if anything—after she died. Eternity was on her mind as she simultaneously stirred the gingerbread batter and scribbled stanzas on a grocery bill.

In my own kitchen, I like to daydream of Emily as one of the first polar explorers. In an intellectually harsh environment, she was brave beyond the perils of thinking for oneself. This particular woman's yearning was, in many ways, still an idealistic girl's longing and curiosity to seek out the cold comfort of knowledge.

Along the way, Emily records sunsets and sunrises, celebrates each season, takes the temperature of her fervour or despair. It was a journey that no one was party to until after her death when Lavinia, in cleaning mode, opened a dresser drawer and discovered the hidden treasure—poem upon poem upon often puzzling poem. Who knew?

When no one was looking, often by candlelight, she composed 1775 poems. This one, written near the end of her life, reads like a memo to the twenty-first century:

> *The most important population*
> *Unnoticed dwell,*
> *They have a heaven each instant*
> *Not any hell.*
> *Their names, unless you know them,*
> *'Twere useless tell.*
> *Of bumblebees and other nations*
> *The grass is full.*
>
> (#1746)

Her beloved friend, Susan, chose Emily Brontë's verse "No coward soul is mine" as a tribute at her funeral. I bow to Emily Dickinson with the inspiration and love I hope this book shows for her life's work. She's the sundial in my garden.

Karen Davidson
Elgin, New Brunswick
June 2022

Acknowledgements

Loving gratitude ...

To Keith, Ellen and Brendan Helmuth, the publishing family at Chapel Street Editions.

To my parents for reading to me, and to my mom for her generosity in paying the tab for books at The Bay or (oh, joy!) Mary Scorer's in Winnipeg; that's how I met Emily Dickinson.

To my adventurous, book-loving cousin, Barbara Hirst, my first reading buddy.

For all the writers' groups I've been part of beginning with the Slaughterhouse Five on Lanark Street ... those gentle souls!

To Kelly Cooper and Jane Simpson who've "heard it all."

And laughed with me.

For Anna Mioduchowska, Edmonton poet and 2004 Banff Centre Writing Studio ally, my poetry lifeline over the past eighteen years. Thank you, Anna.

To my three sisters, Donna, Peggy and Colleen.

To Kenny and Irene Davidson, and the dear memory of 509 Clandeboye Avenue.

And finally, to our children and Warren, beloved late husband:

> *I have no life but this*
> *… except to this extent—*
> *the Realm of You.*
>
> *Emily Dickinson #1398*

About the Author

Karen Davidson's poems have been published in various periodicals, including *Grain*, *Herizons*, and *The Fiddlehead*. She is the author of two previous poetry books, *Windows* and *Jewelweed*. Her book, *Baby's Garden*, was published by the

Early Childhood Centre at the University of New Brunswick and selected for distribution in the province's Born to Read program. She lives near Elgin, New Brunswick in a century-old farmhouse overlooking the headwaters of the Kennebecasis River.

Photo by
Stefan Davidson